T0171622

Poems of Hope, Inspiration & Power

Hazel B. Belk

BALBOA.
PRESS
A DIVISION OF HAY HOUSE

Copyright © 2012 by Hazel B. Belk.

All rights reserved. No part of this book may be used or reproduced by any means, graphic, electronic, or mechanical, including photocopying, recording, taping or by any information storage retrieval system without the written permission of the publisher except in the case of brief quotations embodied in critical articles and reviews.

ISBN: 978-1-4525-5283-5 (sc)
ISBN: 978-1-4525-5284-2 (e)

Balboa Press books may be ordered through booksellers or by contacting:

Balboa Press
A Division of Hay House
1663 Liberty Drive
Bloomington, IN 47403
www.balboapress.com
1-(877) 407-4847

Because of the dynamic nature of the Internet, any web addresses or links contained in this book may have changed since publication and may no longer be valid. The views expressed in this work are solely those of the author and do not necessarily reflect the views of the publisher, and the publisher hereby disclaims any responsibility for them.

The author of this book does not dispense medical advice or prescribe the use of any technique as a form of treatment for physical, emotional, or medical problems without the advice of a physician, either directly or indirectly. The intent of the author is only to offer information of a general nature to help you in your quest for emotional and spiritual well-being. In the event you use any of the information in this book for yourself, which is your constitutional right, the author and the publisher assume no responsibility for your actions.

Any people depicted in stock imagery provided by Thinkstock are models, and such images are being used for illustrative purposes only.
Certain stock imagery © Thinkstock.

Printed in the United States of America

Balboa Press rev. date: 06/13/12

Contents

Section 1: Hope Poems

Section 2: Inspiration Poems

Section 3: Poems of Power

To
My husband, Warren, who has been my helpmate
and encourager for sixty-seven years, and to our son,
Larry, who has been a helper and encourager to
both of us. He has brought us much happiness.

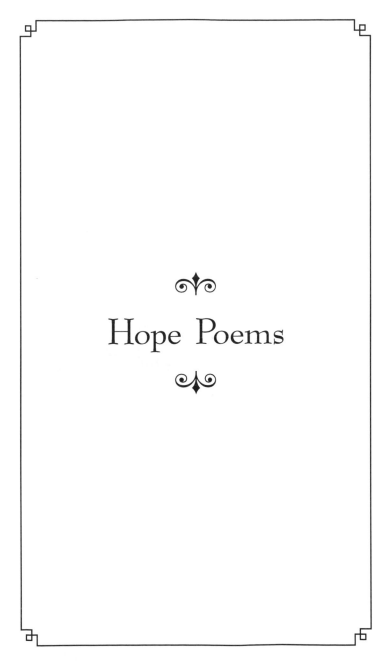

Hope Poems

A Book

I have often thought that
I would like to write a book.
Where it would set on a library shelf
Or in a bookstore nook.

Book lovers would open it up and find
Pleasure, Knowledge and Fun
On pages written before their time.
The 20's 30's and 40's are full of
Memories left behind.

I love to read about writers
Who lived in the 1800's.
They believed and wrote about God
With a serious message
Everyone could Plunder.

A Good Leader

I like a leader who is not afraid of making a decision
A good leader is one who can be trusted.
Everyone can depend on his honesty.

He has the knowledge and ability to
Recognize a problem before it occurs
He has the strength to see that those he leads
Will cooperate with every effort to bring to conclusion
Any decisions that have been made.

In doing this, a leader has the power of a good leader.
We need more good leaders in our nation's government.
May God bless our leaders and keep our nation
Free and under Him

Awaiting the Sound of the Trumpet

Until we hear the sound of the trumpet
God wants us to obey Him.

So much wickedness and violence abound
Caused by Satan.

We need to guard our heart
That we do not fall into his trap. *Matthew 24:12*

Christians need to find a church
Where they may worship with other
believers. *Hebrews 10:25*

Worshiping is inspiring and gives
strength for another week.
Continue to be hopeful which is our strength. *Titus 2:13*

Make Christ known to others
Many have never heard about Jesus
Christ. *Matthew 24:14*

A Lady

A Lady is not only a woman but
One who loves God.

God created the first man, Adam, and said
"It is not good for him to be alone."

While Adam was asleep, he took a rib from
His side and made a woman.

She was made not to walk over him,
But to walk beside him as a helpmate.

She was to become the mother of his children
And to teach them about God.

God named her Eve, and she was blessed.
If all women were ladies,

What a wonderful world this would be.
With everyone knowing and loving God.

A Gentleman

A Gentleman is more than a man.
He is kind, thoughtful and admired by a Lady.

He is polite and opens a door for her
and sees her safely inside.
No one thinks highly of a man who
thinks only of himself.

He honors his parents not because they cared for him,
But because they taught him how to be a gentleman and

How to love and serve God.

Hope

We feel power when we hope
With our feelings of hope

We can always cope.
With any worry or problem

In our lives, our hope
Continues to survive.

We have hope when
We are thinking of someone.

With hope we can continue
Our work or fun.

Hope gives us dreams
of our future.

The Holy Spirit

The Holy Spirit is like the wind,
I cannot see Him but I know He is there.

He touches my heart and I can feel His presence.
Like the wind lifts a leaf,

He lifts me to heights unknown.
He takes me to places I would never go alone.

Just as the wind moves the dead and fallen leaves
To shield the plants from the cold of winter,

The Holy Spirit moves me to know that He is there
To shield me from the storms of life.

And when I fall without a purpose
He reminds me that I am His and He will always

Guide me along life's way.
Jesus promised a Comforter to stay.
He is in my heart today.

Thanks of the Elderly

For a new day
For legs to walk - walker
For arms to work -strength
For eyes to see -eye glasses

For ears to hear - hearing aids
For the ability to cook - food to eat
Thanksgiving dinner -from family and friends

For a comfortable home
Furniture, TV & Radio programs,
Music - Records and cassettes
For family friends and neighbors
For Church family and

All of God's Blessings.

Mr. Snowman

You stand there in the snow
Wearing only, hat, scarf, and gloves.

Children love to play with you
By throwing snowballs at your toes
Hoping to make you fall.

You will probably melt before that happens.
You seem to be enjoying every minute of your short life.

Your mouth turns into a wide smile,
As you take a puff on your cigar.

You have no serious problems,
Just continue to take life as you are.

Rainbow Message

Today I watched a rainbow
Fill the sky with pleasant hues

I tried to choose a color
That would best match my shoes

Then I noticed as I walked nearer
Every color seemed to reflect

It's beauty for my tootsies
I never did expect.

For the message the rainbow proclaims
Is a promise so sincere.

Then I began to realize,
That when I see the rainbow appear;

Thankfulness should be the wish I have
And not a color for my apparel.

The Special Gift

I looked and looked for s special gift
For someone nice as you
The more I thought and the things I saw
Were nice but just wouldn't do.

So will you accept this small little bill
As a token of my desire to express
Thanks to a friend for being so nice
To everyone you will bless.

Faith

Faith is a wonderful thing to have.
It means you have confidence
to believe and trust
in something that is pure and Holy.
This kind of faith
does not require
any proof or evidence.
It is there and you know it.

The Value of Time

The Days go by
So Fast, So Fast,
It makes my head just spin.

To think that time
Is past, Is past
Another year older again.

New Year's Prayer

Open my eyes to beauty
Open my lips to song
Open my mouth to
Speak thy truth,
This whole day long.

Open my mind to wisdom
Open my thoughts to care
Fill me with strength
To work for Thee
This entire New Year.

Friend

A Friend is one who loves
One who has compassion.

He gives of himself to others.
Neither is he selfish.

He shares his time and is happy to
See his friends well and Happy.

Our best friend is Jesus.

Bless the Children

Bless the little children Lord
They are precious in your sight.
Let those who are parents and caregivers
See and provide every need each child requires.

So that they may grow in wisdom, strength,
Body and mind.
Who knows except you Lord
The wonders they may perform?

Doctors, nurses, teachers, scientists
And leaders of all kind.

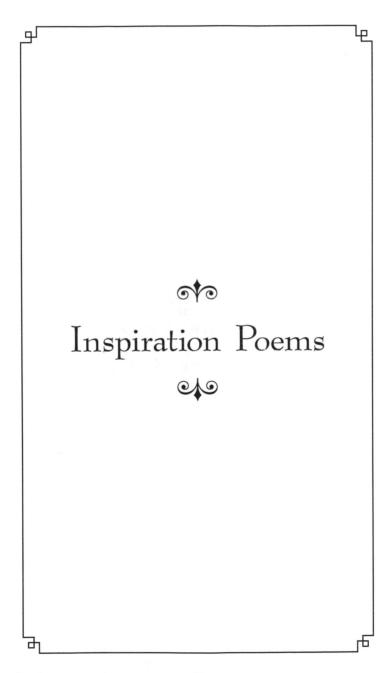

Inspiration Poems

Never Alone

Lifting my heart to Heaven Above
And thinking of God on His Throne
I feel His presence ever so near
And know that I am not Alone.

Speaking His Name In A tone of Love,
He answers, "I am here".
This Presence I'll cherish
Above all earth's wealth
And forever I'll hold it dear.

My prayer today is for God up above
Always to answer my voice
With His presence forever
To fill me with Love
and my heart will forever rejoice.

My Strength

Would I dare begin a day
Before I bow my head and pray
To God for strength and loving care
And in my prayer
For guidance in a world of lust
For faith to look up and in Him trust
Temptations arise within my heart
"Get thee hence Satan"
And I have a new start.
He is constantly reminding me
Of my duty I cannot see.
Daily I drop on bended knee,
Dear God, my strength, my guide
Is my plea.

After the Rain

When it rains we may get despondent and blue
But when the rain ends, the sun can shine through.

The fragrance of the after-rain is a wonderful delight.
Makes one want to sing of the gift of smell and sight.

The ground is damp with a watered lawn
To make flowers grow and the trees to grow tall.

We are blessed from Spring until Fall.
May we thank God for all our blessings.

Growing Old

Each day and each moment is precious
When one is growing old.

Nothing is taken for granted
When each hour is precious gold.

Advantage of every blessing is taken
Because we know they will not last.

Time on earth is limited for God needs us to serve Him
Each day as in the past.

Golden Years are precious when aged we are,
We trust God to care for us

Until we reach Heaven afar.

Amazing Flowers

The purple crocus
first to open their bud,

Along follows the yellow daffodils.
Then come the red and yellow tulips
To dress my lawn.

Next the lovely Iris open wide their jackets,
As if to sing a song.

The camellia and azealeas are waiting
To show their colors of red and white.

It is amazing how each flower has a time of its own
to bloom in our garden.

A lovely picture of flowers for our enjoyment.
Praise God for the beauty of the earth,

And my desire to plant a flower garden.

God's Valentine

You are an angel sent from Heaven above
To take care of your brothers and sisters
who need your care and love.

You are God's special Valentine
who helps those in need

You come to see me often relaxed and jolly
To see if we are feeling fine

Your visits are so special, we are blessed
To have a friend like you.

We shall always remember and love you
You are God's Valentine.

This poem is written in honor of our friend, Judy Matthis. We met Judy in 2001 at the hospital at their Heart Rehab program, for patients who had open Heart surgery. We both were patients eligible for this program. Judy's father was deceased and her mother passed away later. Judy has been visiting us almost every month since then. We are claiming her for our adopted daughter. So many gifts, cards and visits make her our valentine.

Reach Higher

Reach a little higher, you may touch a cloud

Climb a little higher, you may reach an angel

If you look downward, you may not be so proud

Looking down brings a feeling of failing

You need to reach higher to grasp your angel wings.

Patience

Patience is holding my tongue when
I'd like to speak my mind.
When I want to say something, I have learned
To keep quiet when my thoughts are unkind

Patience is doing my work
While others are goofing off.
Knowing that they are foolish and
To me the boss will not scoff.

Patience is waiting for a stop-light
Or a train to pass by.
This is for my safety and could save my life.

Patience is a character trait, therefore
Seek friends with patience

My Cup Runneth Over

I woke up this morning
The sun was shining bright
My cup runneth over.

After thanking God for a new day
I hurried into the kitchen to get breakfast
My cup runneth over.

I thanked God for all these blessings
My cup runneth over.

Then I thanked Him again
For my cup
That continues to overflow.

My Prayer

Bless me now, o Lord I pray
Give me strength for this new day.

I try my best to live for You,
Many today are so untrue.

I need your love to see me through
All the things I plan to do.

Thank you for all You do to bless me
With Your presence.

Mystery of the Wind

I cannot see you
But I know you are there.

I do not feel your touch
As I sit here in my chair.

I hear the rustle of a tree branch
Across my window pane.

I see trees bowing to you
Not seeming to complain.

You are lifting snow
From the housetops all around.

Every now and then you stoop
To take some off the ground.

You may not know
That you are a comfort to me

Though your actual self
I cannot see.

For through the bowing trees
And flying snow.

God is to me saying
"I make the wind blow".

Walking With The Lord

Place your hand in mine
Let's take a little walk,
You are mine and I am yours
We don't even need to talk.

Our hearts are close together
Our souls are intertwined.
No matter how rough the weather
I always seem to find,
That I need to feel the Presence
Of the Spirit Divine.

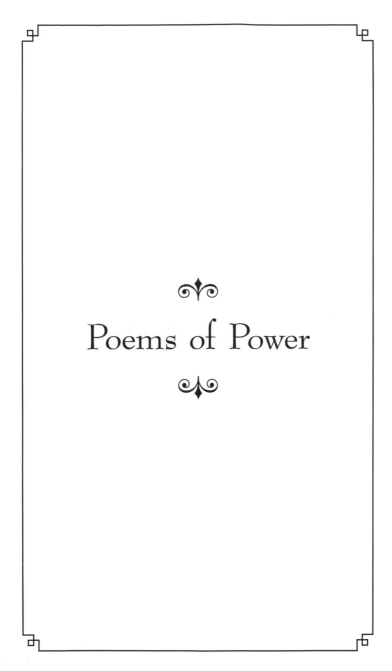

Poems of Power

Roads of Life

There are many roads A- Winding
Across this way called Life

One road leads to a destiny
That ends up in strife.

One road crosses a flowing river
Where blues are left behind.

One road where dreams wind down
To let me hear in my mind

The sounds of music and soft voices telling me
That I am on the right road Home.

The Caregiver

I am a caregiver though no one thinks I am.
I cook meals every day and clean house.

Of course the laundry has to be done
Once a week or more when needed.

There is plenty to do in a household,
But I am well blessed, cooking is a hobby.

Lucky for me, I guess. Entertaining and
Decorating come naturally.

I enjoy being a caregiver. If I live long enough,
Someone may be caring for me.

I would rather be a caregiver.

A Choice

There are times each day when we need to make a choice
What will I have for breakfast? Is
one of the first choices.

How will I use this day to serve God
Will I choose to "Seek first your Kingdom"

See everyone I meet as a brother or sister
And treat them with love and respect?

As your child, I will grasp every opportunity
To tell others of your love and care.

Men in Service

Each day is begun with revele
Up early and to their task

Commanding officer delivering commands
Of course, he too, was once given orders

Just as each new soldier must do
To serve and keep our country at peace.

Let us keep each service man in our prayers
For health, safety and willingness to serve

Stars and Stripes

What a beautiful sound
Each time we hear the song

"OUR NATIONAL ANTHEM"

How lovely the sight
Of the AMERICAN FLAG

As it flies over the Capitol
To let everyone know

That America stands for freedom
Peace and love to all mankind.

I Wonder

There is a wonder about this world
That I don't Understand,

How God made the birds and bees,
And included me in His Plan.

Of all the people on this earth
Why *am I a special one?*

*To live and breathe and enjoy life
Each day from sun to sun?*

*There are many things that I cannot explain
But there is one thing I Know;*

*To trust and believe in God and His word
Is a bliss of Heaven below.*

The Robin

I watched the mother robin build her nest
Then she laid her eggs to rest.
She sat upon them and rolled them under her breast.

It seemed no time at all until they were hatched.
She hovered over them until they were dry.
Then she and her mate took turns feeding the little guys.

There were three of them begging for food,
Three fuzzy chicks waiting for food.

Then one afternoon a storm arrived
SUDDENLY with heavy winds and rain.

I thought mother robin was hovering over them again
To keep them dry.

Next morning I checked on them and saw no movement
In the nest. On the ground below lay one baby bird.

A mother robin was looking around on the ground
Grieving for her chicks.

Life is cruel to birds as it is sometimes to people.
But we have been promised the love
and care of our Heavenly Father.

Looking Through a Glass Darkly

Oh, where have all the years gone? The
days, the months, the hours?
The minutes tick off so silently,
leaving me with little power.

For I sense opportunities gone that cannot be recalled
Age has replaced them with wishes.

Wishes that I could tell all young people to
Listen to your hearts, and the word of God as he speaks

Through Solomon, the King, as his words ring in
The Bible, God's word, found in *Ecclesiastes 12:1*

Inner Peace

The thought of my life led by a guide
Who is sure steadfast and strong.

Though I am small, though I am weak,
He leads me and keeps me from wrong.

Though I may stumble or lose my sight
He lifts me and makes me see,

That He is my shepherd, that He is my light'
That He is living in me.

That He Is living in me.
That He is living in me.

A Farmer's Happiness

A good night's sleep and breakfast waiting at the table.
Your friends all able to help with the corn shucking.

A pond in which to fish and sons to help you plow.
Daughters to help you milk the cows.

A vegetable garden producing a good supply
Enough to share with neighbors as time goes by.

A hard's day's work and a good night's rest
And God to give you peace.

This is everything a farmer needs
To call it happiness.

Finding Peace

Where can I go to find peace of mind,
To my best friend or my minister, kind?

No, there is no person that can help.
Only God has the answer to help you feel peace.

Go to Him in Prayer for He is the One
To calm all your fears.

Give Him your trust and your sincere Love.
Then He will be with you through everything

Forever.

About the Author

I was born in Danville, VA. and at 3 months old, my parents moved to Kannapolis to be with family. I graduated from High School with a Business Diploma and went to work for a local company for 6 years. I met my husband about two years before World War II began. We became engaged and decided to wait until after the war to be married.

The war lasted four years and after he was dismissed from the Navy Air Force in December of 1945 we were married. I have lived in Kannapolis, NC all of my life. I started writing poetry in my thirties. I am now ninety and still find time to write poetry. I attended a business college as a review of my business degree. Then I worked 25 years as a secretary. I have always been active in my church as a leader and a Sunday School teacher for fifty-four years. All of my poems are inspirational. My husband of sixty-seven years has always encouraged me and has been my helpmate. My goal is to share a book of my poems with my family and friends. I have had many hobbies including home-making, cooking, entertaining, crafts, sewing, poetry and reading.

Printed in the United States
By Bookmasters